DRAGONS IN
THEIR PLEASANT
PALACES

For Bruce Bennett

DRAGONS IN THEIR PLEASANT PALACES

Peter Porter

Oxford   New York

OXFORD UNIVERSITY PRESS

1997

Oxford University Press, Great Clarendon Street, Oxford OX2 6DP

Oxford New York

Athens Auckland Bangkok Bogota Bombay Buenos Aires
Calcutta Cape Town Dar es Salaam Delhi Florence Hong Kong
Istanbul Karachi Kuala Lumpur Madras Madrid Melbourne
Mexico City Nairobi Paris Singapore Taipei Tokyo Toronto

and associated companies in
Berlin Ibadan

Oxford is a trade mark of Oxford University Press

First published in Oxford Poets
as an Oxford University Press paperback 1997

British Library Cataloguing in Publication Data
Data available

Library of Congress Cataloging in Publication Data
Porter, Peter.
Dragons in their pleasant palaces / Peter Porter.
p.   cm. — (Oxford poets)
I. Title.   II. Series.
PR6066.073D73   1997   821—dc21   96-44450
ISBN 0-19-288028-4

1 3 5 7 9 10 8 6 4 2

Typeset by Rowland Phototypesetting Limited
Printed in Hong Kong

And the wild beasts of the islands shall cry in their desolate houses, and dragons in their pleasant palaces. . . .

Isaiah, 13:22

ACKNOWLEDGEMENTS

Acknowledgements are due to the editors of the following periodicals and newspapers in which some of these poems first appeared: *The Age*, Melbourne, *Agenda*, *Epoch*, *Eureka Street*, *The London Magazine*, *The London Review of Books*, *New Poetry Quarterly*, *New Writing 4* (British Council), *Poetry Chicago*, *Poetry Review*, *Salt*, *Times Literary Supplement*, *Ulitarra*, *Verse*, *Westerly*.

Again, this collection of poems owes most, or its author does, to The Literature Board of the Australia Council, whose four-year Category A Fellowship supported me while they were being written. This money bought the necessary time to complete the work which went into the book.

CONTENTS

KINGS AND MESSENGERS

Someone, leaning out, said Look it's what
We call the Learning Curve and bang the freight
Shifted in the back and whiffs of hot
Macadam wafted in: I saw my chance
And shouted at them all, No need to wait,
A dream's imagination's ambulance.

That's when the Kafka rules took over—we
Ate aphorisms like porcini, wrote
Our paradoxes as love-letters, free
In their compulsive intellect of all
Simplicity, and what we chose to quote
Was back-street grovelling by a prodigal.

The rushing messengers disowned their kings
But relished livery: they had the Arts
For ukase, scams and heists and stings
To keep them modern, and appraising thoughts
Of sex and synergy, their counterparts
Successive saviours at besieged airports.

A GREAT RECKONING IN A LITTLE ROOM

As I wake from sleep I see
the shape my body makes upon the bed.

It's the on-her-side posture
my cat adopted at the Vet's

when supine from a sedative
she waited the injection in her heart.

It can be stamped as art—Maderno's marble
effigy of Cecilia in the cistern.

Better to see it as the foetus caught
by amniocentesis before birth.

Thus first or last we settle on our side
avoiding Heaven and its avatars.

A summary of life's allusiveness,
out of one dream, attending on another.

When she he mourned had guided him beside
The cliffs and gates of courtship long ago
And ghost-like by the sea which howled below
Her form had surged and eddied with the tide,

When birds whose names both knew still multiplied
In makeshift air around, and counterflow
Of cloud and leaf-light once more set aglow
Her cheeks and nurtured his defensive pride,

He came back to his desk and framed in words
Those elegies in which his world lay wrecked,
His New Year songsters changed to mangled birds,

And still to show him what life cedes to art
Remorse kept house with her safe in his heart,
Her pets all killed or dead from his neglect.

He knew he would be great
  And told his tutor so
But lots of second-rate
  Ramshackle lines 'to go'
Like pizzas on a plate
  He ordered up: we know
His Hardy phase, his Yeats.

But as we sort out from
  The country metaphors
(That almanac birdsong,
  Those Edward Thomas spores)
The few bits which belong
  To his mature scores,
We smell death on the Somme.

He didn't write of war
  But just like Isherwood
Saw straight sex as the flaw
  Which cost a decade's blood—
His poems should restore
  A world before the flood,
The cooked renew the raw.

NATIONAL SERVICE

My childhood watchword—what could that be but Duty
Though my uncles made it a pure rhyme for booty?

I appreciate now that our family was unknowingly modern,
Good Australians, though of the line Hastings to Culloden.

But they never gave a thought to the UK as Home.
Three more uncles are buried in France, and all hated Rome.

Their Nationalism was unconscious, more like Red Neckery,
But they were townees, no truck with bush, bull or peccary.

The Poms were funny but you answered their bugle call:
The mills of Manchester and Oldham had my father in thrall.

We had one Yankee in town, an osteopath named Con,
And Oscars and Giulios in the ranks of Doug and Don.

I wasn't told at the time I'd be classified *Empirish*
Since no part of my ancestry was in any way Irish.

Playground language was barefoot, crude and near,
The very tongue which had nurtured Shakespeare.

Variant dialects: in Brisbane the dunny was 'the dub'—
They did The Lambeth Walk at the Peninsular Golf Club.

My grandfather served Davis Gelatine after leaving The Customs
    House.
He looked like Bernard Shaw but was timid as a mouse.

My mother had the guts, the sassiness, the gloom,
She showed me how terror could fill up a room.

Uncles were tight enough, but aunts were closed purses.
Our Protestant family trusted only Catholic nurses.

The Japs came, the Yanks came, eventually Sex came.
The expense of spirit was OK, but not the waste of shame.

They never called me up but I did my National Service.
The myths of a country conceal where its nerve is.

I moved on: I live in London: I'm grown quite mannerly.
But death will put me on the tram to Annerley

And I'll look out for the familiar sign on the shop
Bushells' Blue Label: I'll have got to my stop.

OLD GOLDFIELDS, MARYBOROUGH

A terror made for midday,
they had walked in galleries beneath our feet
through tinted naves of clays and quartz
five miles and back to Maryborough
and hardby vents and blowholes seen the pulleys
raising ore through Roman arches
and the spacious graveyards fit for those
who never could feel safe in only air.
And now stout Hattie, energy's own dog,
is on the wrong side of the underworld
scouting at the creek's torn barbican
to sniff to life the latest of lost worlds.

Down such a rabbit hole
the Nineteenth Century lured our grandfathers
and great-grandfathers—

gold made sense
of leaving home, entitled all who hate themselves
to test the power of fortune: impervious gold
was a gem in destiny, and all along
a parliamentary Nature was on hand
to clean the mess up. For fifty years
the earth lay gashed by hopefulness and built
a sort of easily assembled Babylon
for these new-minted Gods—today
some sixty souls are forum for the trumpet
of its silent Judge.

When Hattie's rambles
take her to the mullock heaps, she skirts
a fossicker with detector and soft hat
looking for the fillings in this skull.

The landscape now
is featureless as scar tissue
though scrub revives wherever water rides
and ghosts of acid-fingered men
hover as hurt roses or the plums
which fall before the sun has sugared them.

BREAKFASTING WITH COCKATOOS

They go well with baroque flutes,
with charity on a stick
and with the tremor of night-stallions
(to give those bearers of bad dreams
their proper gender)—they incline
a head above their fodder and warn us watchers,
this is not Grace but cantilever greed,
dribbling being nicer far than gratitude.

They defy us to be other than anthrop-
o—is it morphic, ludic, metric?—
cockatooness is unknowable
and consider the only tool we have for an assessment—
wheelbarrow words, rejigged, resprayed
but stationary on the superhighway
whose all roads lead to CD-Rom.
You photograph our souls, they say,
and what you get is quite a pretty plate
fit for The Book of Venerable Beards.

Now, as a gulp of tea goes down my shirt,
I sight a sulphur crest imposed
on Byron's pompous helmet and know
this bird would see no point
in liberating Greece. But wings are shadows
under which a million deaths are waiting
extraterrestrially to be born.

Birds will by Boyds,
beheaders of the worm voyeur
and snatchers of unguarded gristle;
they have platformed, so we think,
Darwinian aeronautics
from where they'll spring to any point
which offers exponential sloth.
They merchandise the proper lines

to front a marble fort embroidered
round the pelvis of a Doge
and when I put my cup down, faced at last
by my long-prevaricated, charismatic toast,
one of my cursory considerers,
non-verbally but colloquially,
pronounces our audience at an end
and offers in exchange a pilgrimage
to decorate a postcard, and I see
the picture in its heart, a true romance,
the embarkation for some special
Cythera of bulging rubbish bins.

MOBILE POOL CLEANER

This is the nation's capital; its pools
May not be blocked by leaves and drowning bees,
And so all day this driven mouthpiece drools
And tide-like sweeps the city's Inland Seas.

Then citizens in whom the moon has hung
A lamp of fear to keep their passions pent
Look down through chlorinated blue, among
The shifting shadows where the light is bent

And see, like Cardinals with conscience, what
Careers and pensions and a good address
Have wrought, and whisper tensely, 'You forgot
To buy the god that goes with cleanliness.'

MEN DIE, WOMEN GO MAD

No ideas but in things, but things
aren't words and understanding clings
to limitation's symbols: the caged bird sings.

Sharks would drown if they ceased swimming:
Cities of God and of the Plain, a twinning
as it was in the beginning.

Within the Book of Self called Commonplace
despair writes libels of disgrace
and Judas/Jesus has a Janus face.

The angel with the lily's at the door,
the cat is terrified, the girl just bored—
'Another thing we can't afford.'

To call my true love to the dance
I need the sonnerie of circumstance
and not the damp disclosures of the Manse.

Men die early, women live on, mad—
it didn't happen to my Dad,
a long life has more reason to be sad.

Vermeer and Donne had eleven children each—
that is, their wives did. D. could preach,
V. paint, with sex and death just out of reach.

We never truly learn to count past one
and hope that when we die we will become
the nothing new under the sun.

DISPLACEMENT

Some would die for a word, some would find
a word only after having planned a death.
John's gospel raked in God, but he came in
number two to his plainsong syllable.
Words are like tonnages, displacement
of existence after settling in a sea
of language. They have their Piltdown grunts,
a history run backwards. A word would give
a party and leave the guests to clean the mess up.

Word me a word says the tyrant, these days likely
to be a Californian behind a cyber-desk;
judge me a word, the judiciary and the press
insist, and press them to death *ex cathedra*;
joke me a word, the communicators in
the nimbussed anarchy joke till the end;
silence me a word or otherwise theory it
assert the reasonable clerks of teaching,
betrayers of their own first love of purpose.

And it was like this when the speculative great
appreciated they could not be absolute,
turning their disappointment on to their own
eclectic brilliance, a Counter Reformation
of conjecture, biting at a Being Beauteous
or a fertile finger. Work and exhaustion
and then metaphor assumed the look of God—
Resto prigion d'un Cavalier armato—
darkness reforming in the gaudy chapel.

THE WESTERN CANOE

We are all in it together, paddling downstream
as in that clip from *Sanders of the River*
but with no one around to shout 'Come on Balliol!'

Undoubtedly here's history in the Steiner sense,
so late into creativity that commentary
gets the prizes, the sexy must of lecturing.

And Bloom's great gun booms heartily
making up for all those snubs, and if he seems
a kosher butcher, at least he's not the Theory Fairy.

In truth, this is a well-equipped canoe,
brother to the Gulf War one, and as attrition
weakens Gibbon, the crew is laser-limning history.

Films are shown on board: *Sophocles' National Service*,
Pico and Vico at the Deux Magots,
Alkan the Alien—but what's so terribly difficult

is starting up afresh. How did they do it, Emily
and friends, out there in the sticks, knowing that a gang
of snobs and clerics had turned the signposts round?

Bliss in that dawn! And if our dawns are chemical
some things never change—a Suburban Sports Reporter
enjoys the engine capacity of a Dickens.

As the canoe beats the rapids to enter the vast
waters of the Eco Pool, drums are calling
for a TV war replete with ice and orphans.

Dangers of shoals and drifting debris, reading habits
of electronic shoppers—and for the academically-inclined
dropping buoys off in The Swamp of Likenesses.

It reminds us of Maurice Bowra cruising the Aegean—
Daphnis and Chloe country for the educated—
and what are our lives but a narrative of metaphor?

Approaching us, a war canoe half The Lady Murasaki,
half state-of-the art modem, and in a dream
the 'Waratah' still on her maiden voyage.

Hot in headphones, brushing off the monkeys,
Mr Kurtz hears what the King of Brobdingnag
told Gulliver. He'll reappear upriver.

Walking with friends along pathways
of a chemically smelly canal
I watch a bright duck break from cover
and then disappear—how banal
its existence, I think, and how apt
for what pastoral Switzerland's about,
a compromise keeping life going
while money sneaks in and sneaks out—
I might as well joke my compliance
and as the duck flaps back in view
let Nature play straight man to Science,
self-consciously say, 'Oh look there,
it's our mallard imaginaire.'

And often in lanes and piazzas
of a village in the Alpi Apuane
I find myself watching and cheering
the local dog Otto, an army
of dogginess summed up in one dog,
a proof to Mankind of its mildness,
of King Stork in league with King Log—
I've little Italian but know that
such lovers of engines and slipstream
are unsentimental and no cat
or dog would be named for an emperor:
beware the Two Cultures debate,
Otto's birthmark's a clear figure eight.

Not far from there in dusty Pisa
where the Campo Santo braves tourists
and art and religion are partners,
I like to check prelates and jurists,

grave notables walled up in stone—
I'm seldom surprised by their calling
though once I was shocked—'Fibonacci,
why you? and why here? What a falling
off for the king of mathematics
to be buried surrounded by all sorts
of fantasists, duds and ecstatics!'
He gloomed at me: 'Series or Ceres,
Death's schooling stops short of world theories.'

Where are the Science Students? Gone to Media Studies,
so why not take the Bible down and get a high
from old Isaiah? Half of what we mean by poetry
is still the rhetoric Hebrew makes in English.
Phasing in a little modern jargon—The Internet,
Pacific Rim, bi-polar wiring—and off we go
back to the full portfolio of lamentation,
the Psalmist's barefoot cries in Askalon,
the Voice of Him that cryeth in the Wilderness
and still breaks wind in Wollongong or Widnes.

The hilltop villages are plangent with goat cries
as water-carts ascend past millet-rows—
stop the bus! this coping stone's an uncle to
reluctance, and *Insh'allah*—where sparrows splash
a generation of fine mercers trained to be
the only hosts a prim cénacle knew—
here Tancred and Clorinda made the closing scene
while ravens, Hittites and black scorpions
catered to the Prophets. These stone museum lions
once were hungry mouths for Ashurbanipal.

As God Eternal joined time in his Mother
phenomena persist of dust collecting in
the sealed mechanism of a watch
and teeth come up decayed. Since figs must ripen
as they did a million years ago, eyes in
the Bible Lands dilate at searing jets
and burning rigs are pillars raised by night—
the very air has purged itself of progress—
such dragons not away on a consultancy
are making inventories of our palaces.

FAT AND SALT

Hear the voice of the pub inside the man
Inside the pub. Millenarian rain falls
Perpetually out of doors, but here
A glaucous injury of spirit finds
Paradise in wit and dying. Names now
Are all of soot and fester; light can't reach
Your eyes until it's passed its millionth spill
Of Guinness, or bowels move you on unless
Pork scratchings salt the freeze-up.
Salt ruin is philosophy: roll on
The body in the case—rational
Researchers gain their temple, minds relaxing
By a bar with afternoons as long
As Milton, and it's true, the world is all
Before us and we need advance no further
Than the clock ten minutes fast forever.
Discipline moves past the wiping cloths,
Dares the bar-high dialectic, averts
Its eyes from pain and contumely since we
Are lost to relevance, playacting all
That's left for courtesy. And we have the shock
Of pier-end museums at our touch,
The monsters under glass, the deviances
Of a far-away Creator: we
Can frame them like home videos—'Moab
Is my washpot, over Edom will I
Cast out my shoe.' The light is deepening,
It's five per cent of content and it won't
Reveal the truth of anything—now pass
The orders upwards—this is the only sort
Of isolation humanity has left,
The subtle chit-chat of self-subtraction,
An inverse Eden rimmed with fat and salt
Whose vacillation's a tautology.

Like the wide-flying Puck of interview
Whose girdle is by CNN and whose
Disposable catharsis gets us through
Our daily fear and boredom, memory
Has dropped its old approach, its panelled lights
And revenants dispensing wholesome guilt,
To be obscene and universal. Time
Has winged the ageing close capillaries
Of this one fearful conscience till plain grief
Has lost its way—not what harm was done,
What crystal pain collapsed in hypo-
thermia or where all hope swam out
To death, but dumb impersonality
May compromise the brutal evidence:
This is the stunted world we have to live in
And I who've ringed the globe five times since that
Eclipse now see myself a frequent flyer
Topping up his helplessness with speed.
The personal is now generic and
To fight this off requires the limits of
An earlier age before a change of hem-
isphere might seem some kind of absolute
When air miles were not banked with hope to make
Anxiety the husbander of harm.
But dreams are twice as fast as Boeings
And visit more appalling shores. The years
Have forced the proper name of love to emulate
Its neuter self. Love is the good which died
That Winter night and with its death became
The wide-winged world—love would be settlement
Of all internal scores—so a mirror holds
The unchanged self beneath its surface,
Happy to exhibit an irrelevance
Of worse and further deeds, knowing what lived
Will go on living until once more

The thin December mist enshrouds the room,
The clock eludes the errant heartbeat and
A closure, like a book put down, defeats
Exhaustion, stepping out of time. Look then
To the great Hobbsean plainness of the world
And hoard its miles against a setting-out.

TOO MANY MIRACLES

Honeycomb-tinted, billiard bald, unblinking,
the baby stretches on his raft of lint—
he is the one quite unselfconscious
thing in a plethora of thinking
and will give his parents no least hint
of what their magic's done or yet will do.
His head is huge, his penis a bold dildo—
the prosthetic ends of life already
exaggerated, our scion of all species
prepares to venture far beyond the steady
proposal of a humanistic thesis
into some overworld—the kin in him,
fancying his mother's breath a zephyr,
knows this is miracle, not synonym.

Where clay foot trod and iron claw dispersed
plants and unctuous animals, a fort
of fragrance hides beneath the ruined grass—
two and a half thousand years have done their worst
to a once civil city and open tombs report
their bodies missing and their souls as well.
Leave the car and find if petrol fumes dispel
the ambience of death: fought-over ground
looks no different from the urban waste
littering the road—here the sherdist found
a crinkly stone and an official chased
the village dogs away. Are they chimerical
these glowing figures who return or is
this just another necessary miracle?

We are not ready for any manifestation
of our special case. But the best of us
eschew conjecture and take by nature from
the gifts encoded in our blood a ration
of hope and then the joy of work—a fuss
of ordered sounds, a roping-up of syllables,
morality of colours, chartered skills—
and far from dark Messapian trappings choose
a sun-kind ripa of philosophy,
as if to die were just to not refuse
a visitable hospice by the sea—
a conch-shell or a goat's horn cornucopia
might spill the face of wonder on the sand,
painstaking painting, miraculous sinopia.

And from the start our baby's being there
will not be pedal note of all sustainable
existence, merely the formula he's given
to make accommodation of the air
and every swarming truth imaginable.
Henceforth equipment matters—tooling up
for universal martyrdom, the cup
which never passes, is his mise-en-scène,
and love and patience and the drip of time
are all apprenticeships. Words intervene
to tell him there exists a far sublime
since there's a word for it: he will discuss
with friends the smoothness of the world and say
too many miracles trouble the meniscus.

THE DEATHS OF POETS

answered some
Of his long marvellous letters but kept none.
—W. H. Auden

It's been a great strain on the words,
they've had to get leave from their journals,
the *Greenpeace* pamphlets, instructions for
setting-up sub-woofers, Satanists' e-mail,
Share Shop panegyrics—
                they're on parade
in their smartly-tailored stiff Obituaries:
they like such gear since obliqueness is in order,
euphemism rules and reading between the lines
is just the sort of secret work they trained for.
                But those who live by words
find words are dry-eyed at the funeral—
there's too much to forgive, the sleight of tongue
which fazed the weak and faxed the managers,
the pity of self-pity as dawn chorus,
imagination's magical deceptions
which kept unfairness grinning like a Tooth
Fairy outed by a child.
                Each meant his life to be
an exemplary success story, but somehow
it all went wrong; death couldn't be postponed,
symposia and Festschriften rotted
among the leaves on crematoria lawns,
hoped-for vindications, complete with jokes
and anecdotes, were never written or
were spiked by teenage editors, while the last
humiliation was the naming of
new names, so up-to-date they featured on
no one's list of enemies.
                Let fashion do its worst,
they said and then it did. Integrity
was no more friendly: when personified

it looked a bully, just the sort who'd say
'I don't like your face' across a bar
or schoolroom, but you knew that really
sniffer glands had found your fear—the fault's
not moral but in talent, and the tunes
which last are driving death from utterance
however tragic its creation: Woodbird sings
and envious good and grieving evil both
are silent.

                And now the words which must
accustom poetry to its lower place
in Paradise are gathering at the wake.
Poetry was fun to write, its veterans intone,
and to be young was very heaven et
cetera . . . and the owl of self-regard
is spotted on the mourning tree, cantos
freely flowing, academic picnics spread,
the young recruits around the swollen knees
of old condottiere, salt hay whispering . . .
time for another et cetera . . . then a tyro says
'Consider Auden's poem where the hero
is a man of action, not a poet
and his letters to his loved one
cannot guess that in a desk this stay-at-home
keeps coded entries in a book whose gulfs
of language change thought's very synapses
which even now both Poetry and Science
must labour to catch up with.'

                The Deaths of Poets
require damp days and a lack of public news
and should be heard of over lunch
or driving to the airport, the latest novel packed,
exchange rate of the lira down—

                Fountains wait, unblocked
of rubbish, cypresses stand to,
and someone's coming with moist hair to bring
you to the house you've always hoped to live in.

JOHN FORD ANSWERS T. S. ELIOT

You knew I was a lawyer, why be surprised
by my distinctive style? Overall, my plays
aren't centred, but what I know of men
tells me centres will form only when
storms erupt to make them. My poetry
is what a lawyer might describe as small
instances growing great occasionally
(that is on sporadic and ingenious
occasions): for this I listened to the manner
men and women, tiring of the means they use
to hide their thoughts or to mislead
their interlocutors, may suddenly,
as philosophers will do, rush into compact
forms of language not malleable
as dialogue—their passions striking them
without advertisement or strategy,
they loop around them such forensic toils
as make pleached gardens out of parkland.
The paradox is poetry, a sort of
versified cascade not requiring metaphor
but like a fountain in a blindfold villa
unmistakably an image of the heart.

Why, three hundred years ahead of me,
you should commend me for belief in love
eludes me. What is there else to write of?
You with the urgings of an impotence
appropriate to your short-breathed age will put
your own adopted crinkle-crankle doubt
into the sort of poetry which won't
assimilate mankind—instead pathetic
Nature and the ramblings of a rhetor God
are called to make your language beautiful.
You are a Psalmist doing without the smell
of burning flesh. Good and evil mixed, you say,

is not the way to justify a knack
with cadencing, and further, I make occasion
fill the cast-list. And here you're wrong
since you resort so often to that arid
concept 'character'. Brutish husbands, vengeful lovers
are simply steeds the words can ride—if every
speaker were the same at each intrusion
on a sentence, then personae might make character—
instead, I write the only poetry
the broken heart has known—not sympathy
for this or that distracted humanoid
but palaces and obelisks and tombs
of diction, and I set before you shapes
with names and callings, sub-contract them to
a place of some malignity and then
I watch. As they come into focus, syntax
stirs and seeks its opportunity:
for this the human race was made, to build
its only lasting Babel, rusticate
the puffed-up feelings and the blemishes
of tragic pity. I have the instrument
to deal with ruined love—to outlast thought
by being before thought what it would say.

BELLINI AND HEINE COME TO DINNER

Did you know that Liszt and his ridiculous woman
read Dante to each other on the shores of Lac Léman
and the consequence is transcendental pianism
and the higher sexuality? Your opinion, Signor Bellini?

I'm afraid, Countess, you have an all too prevalent view
of the Italians, and I cannot properly blame you.
So many of my compatriots are opera factories,
industrious but coarse. I missed your point, Herr Heine.

It is the German genius to make the Devil a conjurer
but beware you Westerners when his scientific,
aromatic tricks are served up by our sorcerer Goethe—
Signor Bellini's mad scenes will all come true.

You are too generous, Countess, when you propose
that I have liberated the caged bird of the soul:
in *Puritani* I see through words to where the eagle
waits behind the sun. You may sneer, Herr Heine.

Why does God waste beauty, whether of limb or visage,
in framing the crooked structure of the mind?
Probably to laugh at their credulity who think
their fortunes fixed. You will die young, Signor Bellini.

The calm before the storm, the calm which follows it,
anyone, Countess, can show us that. It is the calm
within the storm which I compose. As for you, Herr Heine,
you are a Leopardi compelled to bark in German.

The Greeks were here before you, Signor Bellini.
Hubris with its false Icarian wings sets out
to find sublimity, but by a shorter route
Ganymede is roped up to the impatient gods.

One encounters strange philosophers at your table,
Countess, but I will leave the last word with Herr Heine.
Tomorrow I go with my belovèd to the country—
no words, no music, only Nature and Love are there.

BROWNING MEETS WAGNER AT THE SCHLESINGERS'

'Once I wrote of Life's C Major; so prophetic!
It was the very time you made your *Mastersingers*.'
'Few poets can read music; none should use such terms.
These wretched key signatures! But we must be neat.'

'Perhaps, but why does German music conquer everywhere?
Professionalism! Technique, not heartwork governs art.'
'Oh, poet, you have never suffered in our theatres—
I long for just one of Bellini's unpedantic tunes.'

'When I look at paintings I behold the Greek
and Jewish worlds in harness. Is this not so?'
'Our Saviour was an Israelite, yet what he brought
about by Jordan was an upsurge of pure blood.'

'But Master, it is only when Euripides
is yoked to Saul that Western eyes are cleansed.'
'They must be baptised, then my loyal Levi
will show the Germans what conducting is.'

'One of our paper hacks has written of your trip:
"The Future of the Theatre meets The Theatre of the Future".'
'Diamonds in the desert! My life has been devoted
to bestowing ritual on Nature's Morning Song.'

'I'm told you read your Shakespeare like so many
breves and semibreves and words become fixed tones.'
'He is the God who rules us all, so when my art
disgusts me I delve instead among his feasting plays.'

'The world as lyric gesture—so many I have known
have ruined love by harping on its ecstasy.'
'Yes, poet, you are right. Even in *Tristan* I
incorporate truthful dialogue, not just as recitative.'

'The Norse Gods die, but good old savage Germany
endures—a slice for each of G Flat Major bliss.'
'But soon the time will come when by a sea or some
wide lake the heart must pause to hear its own lost song.'

COLLATERAL DAMAGE

'Beethoven was an ugly man, short of stature, with a pock-marked face cut by blunt (or clumsily-guided) razors, and in his late years with a body-odour strong enough to empty the largest table at any of his favourite Viennese restaurants.' —John Deathridge, *TLS*

I see it this way, Mr Beetfield,
you can't do anything that's true pin-point,
there's always one shot goes astray
and some poor thing that got in range
has to be apologised for when damage
is assessed, with all the pictures in.

And minims, liver-spots on God's back-of-hands,
are disappointment's fine embellishment:
the café empties like a concert hall
at such reiteration, and that wretched frame
the pianoforte's a mechanical lyre
for each new Orpheus with attitude.

Exactitude, as I insisted, Mr Beetharvest,
has its price. I mean any farmer knows
breeding is selection and half a herd
can feel the fall-out. That loaves and fishes draught,
well, you couldn't do it if you had to say
No to factory farming. God gives the means.

Music is prosthesis, the jutting-out of truth
beyond performers' fingers.
Because it makes no difference when we're dead
the extraordinary must be fashioned now,
the impossible made sane ambition
and the body a crucifixion of the mind.

It's as if we're in two parts, Mr Beetsugar,
like that guy Montaigne wrote—imagination
puffs us up and reality deflates us.
When the vet said this won't be a healthy calf,
if I'd believed him I'd have lost
a square-eyed runt became my best milk-giver.

The bombardment lingers in the air
as octaves, and the awful pain of deafness
still resonates above the stave.
Looked at another way, a youthful virtuoso
tells his mistress he mustn't marry
having already composed her rejection of his love.

I'm an amateur of ballistics, Mr Beetweevil,
and I don't value megadeath or even
cluster bombs and shrapnel. The point of God
is perfect aiming, something we can't do
on earth. And yet it seems our progress,
as we call it, comes from near-misses.

Darkness visible—perhaps, or
silence audible—or crowding
immeasureability in a phrase.
The silent piano weeps on earth—
time rots in Heaven, ignoring
the *fingerfertigkeit* of angels.

FAFNER'S NEEDLEWORK

I wanted to control the universe
but now I'm buried in a mass of notes
and night by night my dreams are getting worse.

That selfish genius took me from a myth
and kitted me out with steam-age harmonies,
anachronisms I can't be bothered with.

So I'm embroidering the history of mankind:
power corrupts etc., and which came first
the healthy body or the healthy mind?

You might say I'm that peerless Trinity,
Das Ich, Das Es, Das Uber-Ich, and who'd
be master must decapitate all three.

And he'll be stupid, natural and cruel,
hear forests murmur and translate their birds,
then challenge me to fight a bloody duel,

Horns v. Tubas. My enchanted gore
will introduce the simpleton to fear
and start the whole shebang up as before.

Let's call a halt—back to my needlework,
bring up the lights, tell the audience to go home
before the music drives them all beserk.

Bayreuth itself is just Beirut freeze-dried
and all that Early Warning Systems do
is sprinkle holy art on genocide.

THE TENOR IS TOO CLOSE

Our tenor's stumpy, stout and spitting as he sings.
No wonder Doriano, who ran for Italy

at the Olympics, whispers to us softly,
'Il povero, che brutto'. Mozart was small

but rather vain of his good looks. The beautiful
we tend to think does well to stay aloof

and just exist. The actions of the world
deliver up like Fabergé

that ruinous perfection Czars desire,
loving most its pointlessness.

So if you aren't a gracious object
(however subject to time's overlay)

you go down coughing mines or boil your eyes
in lapidary drilling, milled with slaves.

While memory continues there'll be art
but think of Heaven where we had

blank space of everything potential
and revelled in iconic nothingness

which childhood was the first to smirch.
One day we'll be adult and then we'll know

that truth is comparable to Shakespeare,
miraculous for being possible.

But distancing stays difficult, so we duck—
the tenor now is right in front of us

and Mozart's notes survive a hail of spittle.
You need, like Doriano, to know you're loved.

A DANCE OF DEATH

The cows sidle up to the fence
    To eye these impeccable creatures
Parading their bold present tense
    And mark upon such worldly features
        The instinct of herds,
        The display of birds,
        The polish of words,
Disbelief held in willing suspense.

The sheep snatch at tussocks of grass
    While watching bright hampers unpacked,
In the theatre a musical farce
    Shows love going down on its back—
        Black tie out of town
        Where bubbly may drown
        A matronly frown—
Troppo Glyndebourne, alas, O alas!

Beasts and humans aren't built to discern
    A dance which extinction has planned,
That whatever it is that they earn
    They're all to be duly trepanned,
        The wealthy donator,
        The TV debater,
        The tone oscillator,
Each one made redundant in turn.

A few vocal decades from now
    This freshly-cut stone will have warmed
And the glories which rich men endow
    By time will be hugely deformed,
        New verities loom,
        New shapes to a room,
        New rites for a tune
And the orbital cropping of cows.

SKINNING A SKUNK

Now there's a taking title. What
Can I who've only once been on
A horse compose in verse to show
My Nature Wisdom: do I know
The latest Georgics, can I pleat
Our ancient art to modern song?
And is my skunk-lore sound? It's not.

But be a Rocky Mountains bard
At least on paper is the urge
As anthropologists whose belts
Of Aztec silver hang with pelts
Of phones and CDs startle birds
By shouting tropes at ocean's verge—
The sky is high and life is hard.

The Grizzly droppings blaze like gold,
What could a city poet say
Of caymen craft or lizard lurch,
Coyote's spoor and condor's perch,
Or even how a stockman gelds
A horse or what vets do to spay
A cat. Stop! Poems must be sold.

And in Australia now they hymn
The last black queen Van Diemen's Land
Sent into exile, and lags who
Joined tribesmen living on grub stew
And baked galah: a native theme
Has critics eating from your hand.
Parnassian suits an interim.

Today the skunks and foxes meet
In litter-bins while dolphins die
In mile-long trawls—it's poets now
Who roam the woods and gild the bough
And banks which skin the vertebrate.
Life changes, but not poetry:
Skunks stink and poets have to eat.

VERDI'S VILLA, SANTA AGATA

Within a radius of fifty miles
round Reggio and Modena
the landscape smells of shit.
Miracles are never kind
and Emilia-Romagna's cooking
is renowned throughout the world.

The sun turns steadily
over the standing fields,
imported Kiwi fruit
replace the orchard crops
and dry-course rivers sleep
below heraldic bridges.

They farmed their art one time
with the same intensity,
and still you see the turbid
fruits of death and nature
in Dosso's boskiness
and buttocks by Correggio.

Where though to find that grand
ordinariness which marks
the few world-eating geniuses?
Great families shrink at last
to names on famous forts
and visits after lunch.

Verdi's villa has every touch
of provincial stylessness—
cramped rooms, dull views,
the decorations of
a Paymaster-General's widow,
glassed memorabilia.

In the garden a sluggish pond,
a tumulus for ice,
rambling paths leading
to a prairie gate
and a melancholy cat
prescribable as noon.

THE LION OF ANTONELLO DA MESSINA

My lion tells me
that the word can kill and will do so
without warning. Together we have
house-trained terror till it's fit
to undertake a miracle for Science.
The underworld of things is Paradise,
the sun in stained-glass portholes made
to adore the laws of its dismantling
and all the books which must be studied
if Creation is to stay on course—
witness then the sheer assemblage
of this quiet; has any other sainted cell
so radiant a cross-section?
Without my lion nothing would connect,
he is the way imagination went
while God was still explaining it.
Antonello can't domesticate
my cauldron of a mind and so
he tidies everything and has the lion state
Jerome is king of thinking beasts.
But to get the entire world into
so small a painting is more than skill,
it adds up to theology.
Of all the lions I've had, this beast
of Antonello's is the most complete;
he lays his muzzle in my lap
as if he knows it is a fearful thing
to fall into the hands of the living god.

WHAT BORROMINI SAW

Something appropriate to being Bernini's butler,
An upstart world of feigning ecstasy,
An inflammatory geometry growing ever subtler,
A foothold of angels on the slope of a pea.

The House of Melancholy as a Temple of Reason,
Concavity, in shape as a recessive gene,
The Mass compressed to just Kyrie Eleison,
Earth's curve, Sky's line, Man in between.

From the latin 'caedo', a stonecutter's suicide,
But loved by materials on scaffold or in hod,
Rome's bridegroom ditched by his hard-faced bride,
The Phoenix Basilisk of an Incarnate God.

THE PINES OF ROME

(For Katherine & Royston)

As ghosts of old legionaries, or the upright
farmers of that unbelievable republic,
the pines entail their roots among the rubble
        of baroque and modern Rome.

Out by the catacombs they essay a contradiction,
clattering their chariot-blade branches to deny
the Christian peace, the tourist's easy frisson,
        a long transfiguration.

Look away from Agnes and the bird-blind martyrs,
the sheep of God's amnesia, the holy city
never built, to the last flag of paganism
        flying in mosaic.

Then say the pines, though we are Papal like the chill
water of the aqueducts, refreshment from a state
divinity, we know that when they tombed the martyrs
        they ambushed them with joy.

Rome is all in bad taste and we are no exception
is their motto. Small wonder that Respighi, 'the last Roman',
adds recorded nightingales to his score *The Pines
        of the Janiculum*.

And the scent of pines as we dine at night
among the tethered goats and the Egyptian waiters
is a promise that everything stays forever foreign
        which settles down in Rome.

Therefore I nominate a Roman pine to
stand above my slab, and order a mosaic
of something small and scaly to represent
        my soul on its last journey.

THE COCKS OF CAMPAGNATICO

The heart grown old can't fake its scholarship
And won't essay that glib insightfulness
Which once it made a moral landscape from:
This village, half its human figures and
Its cats and dogs enthroned in windless sleep.
Law's brutal now—a German bus deep-parked,
A gang of no-ones-in-particular
Kicking to death a pigeon—how may they be mapped?

Only within the self can scales be hung.
Ignore mere detail says the ageing conscience,
Encourage emblems any mind can hail.
And so the roosters of the valley stir
As if to answer such a challenge, though
They're late, their tubs of sun already full,
And beautifully redundant to themselves
Propose and repropose the Resurrection.

Where may I take my now imploded body
To encompass vanities outside itself
That calming all its spasmic platitude,
Its counting days to dying, miming health
As if it woke each morning in a pot
On a dry balcony and felt the wind with stealth
Approach, it might for once appear at ease?

Only some site where grief has entertained
A lifetime's certainty could host such grace,
A tumulus of constant living, veined
By hope and its humiliations—here
Along the slopes which lead down from the hill
Of Saint Sabina's Wedding Saturdays
Where Aventine internees prosper still.

A great unswervable unfairness of
Well-off with poor, long-life with death, despair
With hope—this is the place Rome handed on
To sequent centuries; the very trees compare
Each person at their feet and measure love
And loneliness as if stalled on a stair
Where saint might doubt or devil cease to tempt.

The Roman Commune on this ground has made
A straggling garden fused with modern roses—
Nearby, the Circus Maximus decayed
To little but a rubbish dump hears cars
Re-echoing its chariots while the bells
Resounding modern couplings can keep faith
With life beyond the silence of monks' cells.

But roses, killed by time, live outside time
And open, fold and blow as if the world
Were just the moment when they come in view,
No different tomorrow, petals whirled
Away by wind but new buds setting fire
To morning when the rim of Rome is pearled
By risen dust encircling milky sun.

Now, in my sixties, I have quarrelled with
My friends, including that old friend, my brain,
And sated with the remedy of myth
Have no resort but using my tired eyes
To reinvent the day—a thousand flowers
Undisciplined but municipal
Vie with St Dominic and the flying hours.

No rose would stammer for a catacomb
Or candle-tinted altar, but repeat
The litany it's rooted in, the round
Of youth, and genuflecting to the seat
I'm on, point at exhausted Rome to prove
Through roar of motorinos time's defeat
Even in this its consecrated heart.

THREE OTRANTOS

The first *Otranto* was my ship.
How yacht-like were those working vessels,
long grey slivers dipping below the waves
through periscopic sights—
born Barrow-in-Furness in the twenties,
ready to carry me docilely
from Hamilton Wharf to Tilbury
in 1951. Down on H Deck
with the hides and green bananas
we rolled in half-light through
seas more imaginary than real—
brandy ten pence a glass,
The Orient Line white jackets of the stewards,
smoked haddock in warm milk,
married women taking off their rings,
a smell perpetually of creosote
and cooking. No more beautiful ship
ever edged the stuffy waters of the Med
or showed the flying-fish
how riding gracefully through waves is done.
Later, among the cabin cruisers of the Thames,
guessing her in the breakers' yards,
I paid my dues: *The Otranto*, I said,
was the true umbilical which linked me to
my never-to-be-known, all-knowing mother.

My second Otranto was all Walpole's,
his gothic castle so unlike
the actual Norman, Angevin
and Aragonese fortress in Apulia.
In my thought it represents the lies
I told and go on telling as a writer.
I traced the progress of the Gothic Novel
in examination papers earning
fulgent marks while never having read

a word of what I praised. Such dubious means
to powerless ends. At least I learned
two things—Horace Walpole was a brave
if over-fastidious man, and Peacock's
Nightmare Abbey and his *Melincourt*
are more fun than the Gothic modes they mock.

The third Otranto's the real site.
In that side-chapel of the Cattedrale
I wondered at the several cupboards
flanking the plain altar—why store crockery
in such a place? Grey utility cups and saucers
stacked behind glass doors. Up close
they proved so many skulls and pelvises and femurs,
a vile Old Mother Hubbard's hoard
of ghostliness. That murder done in 1480
should look so pointless with its faith
and courage drained away was shocking to
my secular and self-decoding mind.
The decapitating blade, in profile like
the Adriatic, hovered in the air.
The smell of sea-food cooking and the sharp
sting of restorers' lacquer brought
the present back. Otranto stretched its arms
to inventory the day. Almost lunchtime
it declared, enrobing ancient martyrdom
in a blue inclusiveness of sea.

A LAMENT

In valleys where winds meet,
in silences of chambers
untouched by the sun,
in tufa uplands and long strata
of the vanished waters,
we will find them—
our salted ancestors
in households still outflanked
by cat and ibis mummies,
the losing parts of ghostliness
not magicked now by moon or stars—
their eyes would sweep forever
super sydera, but that they have no eyes
nor ears, but only a long nothingness
imagined by the gods.

In dreams they visit us
but it is our lives which are
their prison. They made their tombs
and temples to invigilate our thoughts
and their dementia is our memory.
Though such messages are fading from us
a chemical exchange goes on—
a dynasty of prayers becomes a waterfall,
a warrior's resting place the chair
of some sand-flooded tractor.

When all the lives which ever were or ever will be
are trimmed like stone and share
stone's magical inertness
winds will still lament the strangeness
which was life and silence look to find
its birthplace in an allegoric music.

And the winds say
What did you do in the war, Daddy?
and the reply, I kept my gas mask on.
Nothing is straightforward
and the shortest distance between two points
may be the way to death,
and gravity is bounced about the rocks
by private zephyrs. The only sound now
is a lift ascending to the floors
of non-existence. They wait there for us,
our friends and lovers recognizable
as we shall be by their perfect missingness.

A SHORT BALLAD OF UNBELIEF

It's not a good time for risk-taking
The baleful brain says to itself.
You're not well, you ought to propitiate
The God who ordains failing health.

But he might respect greater defiance,
No whimpering crossing the bar,
The Atheist's Comedy playing,
The invite marked 'come as you are'.

Have they found what they looked for, those faces
Whose names are now washed off their stones?
Do their mounds keep them warm out of Domesday,
A permanent summer of bones?

You might toil up precipitous stairways
To visit high altars and tombs,
Find Maria d'Aracoeli is worth it,
Love shrunk to a handful of rooms,

But nothing can prove your existence
Will keep going after you're dead.
You may think that it's owed you—for instance
That Paradise looms in your head

And millions are born to ensure
Creation should lead on to you
With all the juridical gestures
Which keep the elect very few.

But can Art and Aesthetics survive when
The body is held at discount
By old age, and hope of survival
Is more of a cringe than a flount?

Will you ever convince your intelligence
To accept the intentional breath
Of frescoes and candles and statues,
The paraphernalia of death?

Unbelief has just enough cunning
To be grateful when nailing the lie
Of transcendence that still every steeple
Points nowhere but into the sky.

A REINTERPRETATION

After the Miracle of the Loaves and Fishes
Was sought the Miracle of the Further Wishes,
That the nurturing of ordinary folk
Should count for more than simply to evoke
A loving god, but daily be set forth
(Because Your Father, slow to come to wrath,
Knoweth ye have need of all these things)
In food and drink and love and cherishings—
Yet like the parables, the miracles
Were too exemplary to be much else,
And ants and birds were drawn to gulp the crumbs
And grass regrow beneath ecstatic bums
And scribes and painters muddy up the scene
With praise of what was just a go-between's
Brief granting of unnatural exemption
The while the dutiful indifferent sun
Content that life on earth had come to stay
Lighted the miraculous and the following day.

IL LACERATO SPIRITO

Refreshment of life
is the principle which damns us all

Nature or Nurture? The lamb trots after its mother
up the ramp and into the waiting ship

Death cannot bear its own company,
it destroys life to go on creating it

The peace of nescience is the dream
of plants and stars and parallel lines

Spirit, being God's intake of breath,
constantly admonishes its maker

Such insubstantiality restricts
Paradise to the interface of time

Emerging unsorted in the world
we have to learn to tolerate our shapes

And that is why the spirit's torn
from the body to be eloquence

So let my cry go out and let my fear
inseminate the numbered elements

MUTANT PROVERBS

Nine stitches are a waste of time.
It's the early worm who gets caught by the bird.
A Mossy Stone gathers a Rolls.
Sleight of hand makes many work.
There's no police like Home.
Space for the goose is spice for the gander.
Butter the devil you know and batter the devil you don't.
The child is farther from the man.
When in Rome do the Romans.
An apple a day is not a doctor's pay.
A friend in tweed is a friend in need.
No fuel like a cold fuel.
Vedere Napoli e poi mentire./See Naples and lie.
Pour encourager les auteurs.
Après le déluge, c'est moi.
Blood is quicker than mortar.
Spokes of the Devil.
In drains begins responsibility.
The family that prays together slays together.
From cleanliness to godliness, what next?
Apotheosis of the dons.
A rose by any other name would cost much less.
A diamond is for Eve.
Jam yesterday, jam tomorrow, logjam today.
Life is a dram.
By their frights ye shall know them.
Dying will be a great invention.
Sweet are the uses of advertising.
Virtue is its own regard.
Our hearts were young and grey.

DEATH AND THE MOGGIE

Good Morning, Citizen Cat,
I am Death who's come
To take you from this flat
Back to where you're from.
Are you ready, Comrade Cat?

Don't pester me, Sir Death,
This is my morning rest
When I forget that teeth
Shred flesh from bone with zest.
I'd fillet you, proud Death.

Stay calm, Signore Gatto,
You have to leave but you're
In that anthology from Chatto
On page 174.
Va' ben, amico gatto.

Listen, egregious Hades,
Those only give you power,
Fine Gentlemen and Ladies,
Who recognize their hour.
Don't mix with rough trade, Hades.

The time has come, Herr Katz,
To chew what you have bitten,
This languor is ersatz;
That you can't stay a kitten
Kein Rätsel ist, Mein Schatz.

I'm not, you Modern Hermes,
Quite ready yet to die.
Though this the end of term is,
I'm still as bright of eye,
A beautiful brown Burmese.
Each star helps light the sky.